Secrets
of
Sport

The Technology That
Makes Champions

James de Winter

Fact Finders is published by Capstone Press,
a Capstone Publishers company.
151 Good Counsel Drive, P.O. Box 669,
Mankato, Minnesota 56002.
www.capstonepress.com

First published 2008

Produced for A & C Black by

Monkey Puzzle Media Ltd
The Rectory, Eyke, Woodbridge
Suffolk IP12 2QW, UK

Library of Congress Cataloging-in-Publication Data

De Winter, James.
   Secrets of sport : the technology that makes champions /
by James de Winter.
     p. cm. -- (Fact finders. Extreme!)
   Includes bibliographical references and index.
   Summary: "Presents the science behind sports including
snowboarding, soccer, and tennis"--Provided by
publisher.
   ISBN-13: 978-1-4296-3113-6 (hardcover)
   ISBN-10: 1-4296-3113-9 (hardcover)
   ISBN-13: 978-1-4296-3133-4 (softcover)
   ISBN-10: 1-4296-3133-3 (softcover)
1. Sports sciences--Juvenile literature. 2. Sports--
Technological innovations--Juvenile literature. I. Title.
II. Series.

GV558.W56 2009
613.7'1--dc22

2008025322

Editor: Cath Senker
Design: Mayer Media Ltd
Picture research: Laura Barwick
Series consultant: Jane Turner

This book is produced using paper that is made from
wood grown in managed, sustainable forests. It is natural,
renewable, and recyclable. The logging and manufacturing
processes conform to the environmental regulations of
the country of origin.

Printed in China by C & C Offset Printing Co., Ltd

Picture acknowledgements
ActionPlus p. 14 (Tony Donaldson); CEDIP p. 10 (2007
CEDIP Infrared Systems); Corbis pp. 4 (Reuters), 17
(Reuters), 18 (Annebicque Bernard/ Sygma), 20
(Schlegelmilch); Equip2Golf p. 12 (Gary Mayes/
golfballtest.org); Getty Images pp. 1 (WIN-Initiative), 5
(John Kelly), 6 left (Mark Nolan), 6 right (AFP), 7 (John
Peters), 8 top (AFP), 11 (AFP), 13 (S. Greenwood), 15
(Shaun Botterill), 16 (Bradley Ambrose), 19 (AFP), 22
(Jakubaszek), 23 (WIN-Initiative), 24 (VEER Elan Sun
Star), 25 (Steve Satushek/Image Bank), 28 (Brian Bahr),
29; Hawk-Eye Innovations pp. 8 bottom, 9; PA Photos
p. 27 (Kirsty Wigglesworth); Rex Features p. 21 (Sipa);
Science Photo Library p. 26 (BSIP, CIOT).

The front cover shows athlete Oscar Pistorius competing
in a 400-m race (Rex Features/Olycom SPA).

Every effort has been made to contact copyright holders
of material reproduced in this book. Any omissions will be
rectified in subsequent printings if notice is given to the
publishers.

CONTENTS

Abbreviations **m** stands for meters • **ft** stands for feet • **in** stands for inches •
km stands for kilometers • **km/h** stands for kilometers per hour • **mph** stands for miles per hour

Snowboard sandwich

It's easy to slip and slide on ice and snow, but to move quickly in the right direction takes lots of practice. In the hands of a skilled rider, a snowboard is fast and easy to control.

Canadian snowboarder Jasey-Jay Anderson carves a turn. Slowing down transfers your energy to the snow and makes it spray up.

Wipeout

If you are moving very fast on a snowboard, it can be tricky to turn a corner. If you get it wrong, it's **wipeout** time!

The board is flexible. It bends as you turn.

wipeout when a snowboarder falls over

There is a plastic layer on top of the **fiberglass** called a top sheet.
Top layer: plastic
Upper middle layer: fiberglass
Lower middle layer: wood
Bottom layer: plastic

You can change the shape of the edges of the board and sharpen them for better control.

The bottom layer is made of a super slippery plastic.

Adding wax to the bottom of this layer makes the board go

faster.

The middle is made of wood or foam to hold the shape and coated in fiberglass for stiffness and strength.

A snowboard is made like a big sandwich by gluing layers of different materials together. Each layer has a special use.

fiberglass material made from very thin, strong threads of glass

Slipper or soccer shoe?

Modern soccer shoes may look like slippers, but they are carefully designed to allow the best possible control of the ball. This is useful when you're hoping to score with a curving free kick.

David Beckham is famous for his curving free kicks.

Stitched not laced

Early soccer balls were laced up, just like shoes. Now they are made from 20 hexagons (six sides) and 12 pentagons (five sides), stitched tightly together to make an almost perfect sphere.

Curving the ball is useful in baseball, too.

For a perfect curving free kick, you have to kick the ball so it spins as it moves forward. The laces on the shoe are sometimes covered by a flap to make it easier to kick a curve ball.

1 To make the ball curve, you need to make it spin.

2 The spinning changes the air flow around the ball.

3 This makes the ball curve as it moves.

4 The faster the ball is spinning, the more it curves.

Hawkeye: The ultimate tennis judge

In tennis matches, the ball moves so fast it can be hard to see what has happened. Arguments break out on the court. "That ball was in!" "No way; it was out!" A new system called Hawkeye could stop the arguments.

Serena Williams can hit a near perfect shot, but even her shots sometimes go out.

Hawkeye can prove where the ball bounced within a few millimeters. Here, the ball hit the line, so it was in.

Eyes of a hawk

Players use Hawkeye during training to help improve their game. It shows them where all their serves and shots landed.

IN

motion   movement

The Hawkeye system uses multiple cameras around the tennis court. They record the **motion** of the ball—which travels as fast as a racing car. From the camera images, computers can estimate where the ball landed. The system is accurate to within a few millimeters.

The player served the ball from here.

A tennis serve can travel at over 124 mph (200 km/h), often too quick for human eyes to see where it bounces.

The ball is out.

The ball landed on the wrong side of the court.

OUT

Snickometer: The cricket camera that sees sound

In cricket, the ball can travel at up to 100 miles per hour (160 kilometers per hour). It may only touch the bat for a few thousandths of a second. It's hard to see or hear exactly what has happened.

When you rub your hands together, you feel them getting hotter. The same thing happens when a fast cricket ball hits the bat. If the ball hits the bat, the spot where it hit will be hotter than the rest of the bat.

An **infrared** camera makes it possible to see the hot spot on the bat.

Where's cow corner?

The fielding positions in cricket have some odd names, including silly mid off, gully, short leg, fly slip and cow corner.

infrared energy that hot objects give off, which human eyes cannot see

The snickometer is a clever device that uses microphones to record the sound as the ball passes the bat. It checks if the ball has touched the bat.

If the ball touched the bat, you would see the peak on the **sound trace**.

If the ball passed the bat but didn't touch it, the snickometer would show there was no sound trace.

sound trace   the picture of a sound on a snickometer

Swing to win:
The perfect golf game

Hit properly, a golf ball can travel nearly 1,640 feet (500 meters) in under six seconds!

Here you can see the inside and outside of a golf ball. The ball is made of a tough outer plastic skin with rubber or plastic inside.

It's not just about hitting the ball hard though. The design of the ball and the accuracy of the swing are vital to being a successful golfer.

What are the dimples for?

Most golf balls have between 300 and 500 dimples. The dimples help the air move smoothly over the ball and make it go farther.

driving   hitting a long distance shot in golf

Although it is small, light, and cheap to make, a modern golf ball is a high-tech piece of equipment.

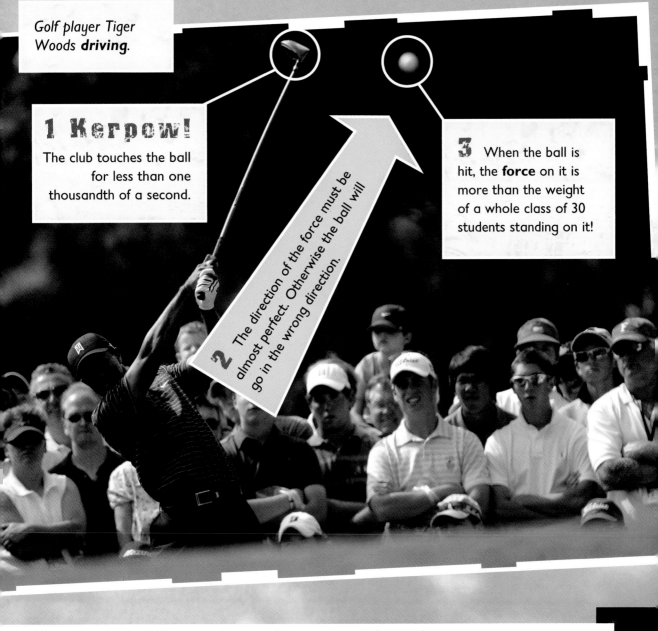

*Golf player Tiger Woods **driving**.*

1 Kerpow!

The club touches the ball for less than one thousandth of a second.

2 The direction of the force must be almost perfect. Otherwise the ball will go in the wrong direction.

3 When the ball is hit, the **force** on it is more than the weight of a whole class of 30 students standing on it!

force a push or a pull on an object, making it move or change shape

Ice, high speeds, and no brakes

Can you imagine sliding down a mountain on a tiny sled, feet first, at almost 87 miles per hour (140 kilometers per hour)? On a luge, you have only a helmet and a skintight suit to protect you.

When you are riding a bike fast, you feel a force on your face and body slowing you down. This is called **air resistance**. If you lean forward and bend your head down, the change in shape reduces the force. It becomes easier to ride. The same idea is used to design things to go as fast as possible.

Wheee!

You don't always need snow. Street luge is a popular sport.

air resistance   the force of air pushing against a moving object

A **STREAMLINED** shape makes it easy for air to flow over the rider, helping him go as fast as possible.

The rider lies **f l a t** to reduce air resistance.

Runner

AIR

AIR

Runner

No brakes!

The luge is one of the fastest winter Olympic sports. The luge has no brakes. To slow down, you push the runners of the sled together.

Skintight outfit further reduces air resistance.

streamlined   with a smooth shape so it can move quickly through air or water

Sprint finishes— won by a nose?

*Horse racing is another sport that has split-second finishes. In athletics, you win if your **torso** crosses the line first. In horse racing, it's the horse whose nose passes first.*

Some sprinters run faster than you can ride your bike and finish the race at almost exactly the same time as each other. Could you decide who won in a split-second finish?

Loser!

torso the main part of the human body from the neck to the top of the legs

It's a **photo finish**. High-speed cameras photograph the end of the sprint race.

Runners-up

In the 100 meters final at the 2004 Olympics, the first four runners finished within 4/100th of a second of each other.

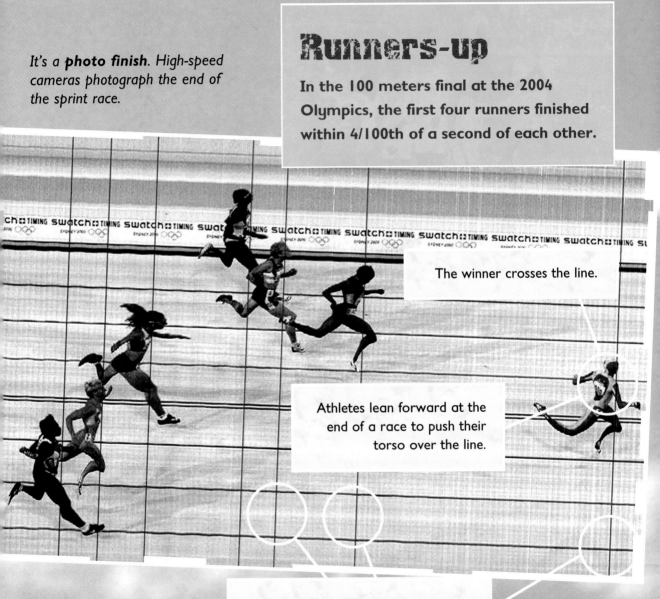

The winner crosses the line.

Athletes lean forward at the end of a race to push their torso over the line.

The red lines show who came first, second, third, and so on.

photo finish   when the end of a race is so close that you need a photo to know who won

Floating a boat

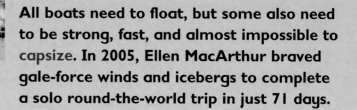

All boats need to float, but some also need to be strong, fast, and almost impossible to capsize. In 2005, Ellen MacArthur braved gale-force winds and icebergs to complete a solo round-the-world trip in just 71 days.

The hull of a racing boat is made from tough materials. A strong, waterproof, outer skin keeps out the water. The honeycomb shape is for lightness and strength.

Make it waterproof

To build a boat, you need the right materials. The **hull** is made with super-strong, lightweight materials. Some useful materials, such as wood, are not waterproof. They are painted or coated in plastic.

capsize when a boat turns upside down   **hull** the main body or frame of a boat

Ellen's special boat was called a **trimaran**.

Ellen MacArthur's boat, before the start of her round-the-world trip.

A trimaran has less contact with the water than a normal boat. This makes the trimaran go faster, but it can be hard to steer.

This very
wide boat
is almost impossible to capsize.

The three hulls help
spread the weight
of the boat.

trimaran   a boat with three hulls

A $35,000 steering wheel!

Formula 1 racing is one of the most expensive sports in the world. Each car costs millions of dollars. Every single part is designed and tested by computer systems to make sure the car is a perfect machine.

A Formula 1 car racing at the Bahrain Grand Prix. This car can reach an incredible 200 mph (322 km/h).

Some racing cars can go from 0 to 100 miles per hour (160 kilometers per hour) in less than 8 seconds.

Pricey

You may only need one of them, but even the steering wheel for a Formula 1 racing car can cost more than $35,000.

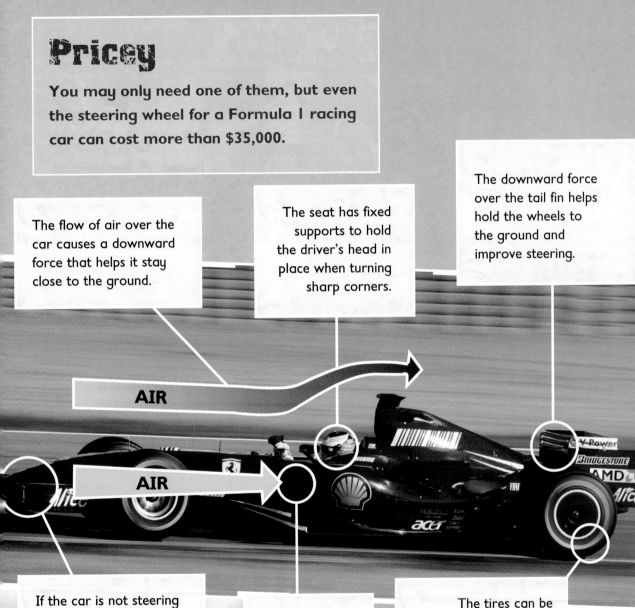

The flow of air over the car causes a downward force that helps it stay close to the ground.

The seat has fixed supports to hold the driver's head in place when turning sharp corners.

The downward force over the tail fin helps hold the wheels to the ground and improve steering.

AIR

AIR

If the car is not steering well, the front fin can be moved during the race to increase or reduce the downward force.

As air passes, it is guided into the engine to keep it cool.

The tires can be changed during the race depending upon the weather conditions.

On your bike!

Whether you're racing or doing tricks, a **BMX** bike can be one of the most exciting ways to move around on wheels without an engine.

BMX bikes are strong and lightweight, with smaller wheels than racing bikes. This makes it easy to race, jump, and move around when they are in the air.

Technical tricks like this take months to learn.

Errr...

Triple tail whip

This is one of the most difficult **BMX** tricks. The rider holds on to the handlebars and then spins the rest of the bike around three times.

grind   a BMX trick where you scrape the axle pegs against a hard surface

Axle pegs are used to stand or **grind**.

Many pedals have studs on them to help your feet grip.

Using triangular shapes in the frame is one of the best ways to increase the bike's strength.

Grooved tires improve grip with the road or track.

It's a boo-wah day: Hang gliding

A **boo-wah day** is a perfect day to jump off a cliff, attached to a hang glider. It's sunny, the sky is clear, and there's a gentle breeze. This is the closest you will ever come to flying like a bird.

Hang gliders can reach speeds over 47 mph (75 km/h) and heights of thousands of feet.

As warm air rises above the cooler air below, it creates an upward force, called lift, that is strong enough to keep the hang glider in the air.

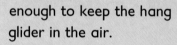

If the lift force is greater than the **weight**, the glider will go up. If the lift force is smaller than the weight, then the glider will go down.

boo-wah day   a perfect day for hang gliding   **weight**   the force pulling objects to the ground

Gravity causes a downward force called weight.

GRAVITY

Warm air provides a force lifting upward.

LIFT

If the upward force is the same as the weight then the glider will stay at a steady height.

Fly me to the Moon!

Well not quite. But in 2001, Austrian hang glider Manfred Ruhmer flew 435 miles (700.6 kilometers), taking the world distance record. It was farther than the distance from Massachusetts to Washington, D.C.

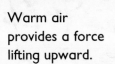

gravity   the force that pulls objects towards the ground

Plug me in! Humans, computers, and fitness

Bigger than you think

An adult's lungs can contain over 1.6 gallons (6 liters) of air. That's enough to fill almost 20 empty soda cans.

Athletes today aren't just found on the track. They often plug their bodies into a computer. Why do they do this?

During most kinds of exercise, you need to increase your **heart rate**. Athletes use special equipment to measure their health and fitness. A portable heart rate monitor is small, light, and easy to use. It measures how many times the heart beats every minute.

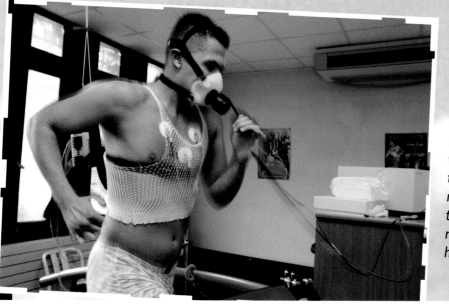

This man runs on a treadmill to test his fitness. He is wearing a face mask to measure how much oxygen he is taking in, and a monitor to measure his heart rate.

heart rate the number of times the heart beats each minute

Athletes measure their **breathing rate** and heartbeat before and after they exercise. It helps them work out how successful their training has been and improve their training plan.

During exercise, the heart and breathing rate will rise.

A sensor in the chest strap measures the heartbeat and sends data to the wrist monitor.

This runner is not wearing a watch— it is a heart rate monitor.

Muscles need more oxygen during exercise, which is why the breathing rate goes up.

breathing rate   the number of breaths you take each minute

The blade runner: Artificial legs

New strong and light materials have transformed sport for some athletes who previously couldn't compete in international competitions.

New, super-strong materials help athletes with a **physical disability** in many sports. Oscar Pistorius was born missing bones in the knee. He had his lower legs amputated (removed) when he was young. His artificial legs are made of a **composite** material that is designed to be strong and light. Oscar is known as "blade runner" because of the shape of his artificial legs.

These sportsmen play wheelchair basketball in special wheelchairs. They are strong, light, and very easy to move around in.

physical disability   condition that means you cannot use a part of your body easily

Oscar Pistorius has two artificial legs. The composite material is springy. It stores energy to help him run fast.

Super fast

Oscar's fastest time for running 100 meters is only about one second slower than the men's world record and faster than the women's.

The curved shape of the artificial leg allows it to bend without breaking.

VISA

58

ndsnorthwest

composite a material made by joining different materials together

Glossary

air resistance the force of air pushing against a moving object

boo-wah day a perfect day for hang gliding

breathing rate the number of breaths you take each minute

capsize when a boat turns upside down

composite a material made by joining different materials together

driving hitting a long distance shot in golf

fiberglass material made from very thin, strong threads of glass

force a push or a pull on an object, making it move or change shape

gravity the force that pulls objects toward the ground

grind a BMX trick where you scrape the axle pegs against a hard surface

heart rate the number of times the heart beats each minute

hull the main body or frame of a boat

infrared energy that hot objects give off, which human eyes cannot see

motion movement

photo finish when the end of a race is so close that you need a photo to know who won

physical disability condition that means you cannot use a part of your body easily

sound trace the picture of a sound on a snickometer

streamlined with a smooth shape so it can move quickly through air or water

torso the main part of the human body from the neck to the top of the legs

trimaran a boat with three hulls

weight the force pulling objects to the ground

wipeout when a snowboarder falls over

Further information

Books

The Amazing World of Sports: The Ultimate Sports Photography Book. Edited by James Buckley, David Fischer, and Ellen Labrecque (Sports Illustrated Books, 2006) A large collection of some of the most amazing sports photographs.

And Nobody Got Hurt: The World's Weirdest, Wackiest True Sports Stories by Len Berman (Little, Brown & Company, 2007) A hilarious collection of some of the oddest sports stories that you might ever read.

The Sports Book: The Sports. The Rules. The Tactics. The Techniques. Foreword by Ray Stubbs (Dorling Kindersley, 2007) More than 400 pages of information about every sport you could possibly think of.

Films

Bend It Like Beckham directed by Gurinder Chadha (Warner Home Video, 2002; PG-13) A comedy film about girl soccer players.

Cool Runnings directed by Jon Turteltaub (Walt Disney Studios, 1994; PG rating), A comedy film about the Jamaican bobsled team and the 1988 Winter Olympics.

Field of Dreams directed by Phil Alden Robinson (Universal Studios, 1989; PG rating) A drama about a Californian farmer who has a dream to build a baseball stadium on his farm.

Web sites

FactHound offers a safe, fun way to find Internet sites related to this book. All of the sites on FactHound have been researched by our staff. Visit *www.facthound.com* for age-appropriate sites. You may browse subjects by clicking on letters, or by clicking on pictures and words. **FactHound will fetch the best sites for you!**

Index